# tulip

**Liz Dobbs**
**photography by Clay Perry**
**consultant Cees Breed**

**Quadrille**

Editorial Director: Jane O'Shea
Creative Director: Mary Evans
Design Assistant: Katy Davis
Project Editor: Hilary Mandleberg
Production: Tracy Hart

First published in 2002 by
Quadrille Publishing Limited
Alhambra House
27–31 Charing Cross Road
London WC2H 0LS

British Library Cataloguing-in-Publication Data
A catalogue record for this book is available from the British Library.

ISBN 1 903845 49 1

Printed in Hong Kong

# contents

# tulipomania

Delve into the history of the tulip and it seems we have always been mad about them. Even before the Dutch experienced the height of their 'tulipomania' from 1634 to 1637, sultans in the Turkish Empire were ordering their subjects to collect thousands of tulip bulbs with which to fill their pleasure gardens. The tulip's history is also the story of many individuals from all cultures and eras who became obsessed with its beauty.

Sometimes the tulip inspired men to do great things – write poetry, plant beautiful gardens, devote a lifetime to breeding the flower – but it also brought out their darker side. In their quest to possess the tulip, collectors bickered, stole, gambled and squandered fortunes, no doubt leaving a trail of misery behind. For some, the goal was to plant *on masse*, to impress people with their great wealth. For others, the desire to possess or create a particular colour or shape in the flower was paramount, and their activities were secret: even one bulb was enough so long as it was the only one and they owned it.

Today, we are still susceptible to the charms of this superb flower. As summer comes to a close, the bulb catalogues tempt us to think of spring colour, encompassing all the jewel and pastel shades in which tulips are now available. In spring, regardless of whatever we are already enjoying in our own gardens, we will be making lists of more 'must-have' varieties for the following year, spurred on by visits to bulb gardens and flower shows. We are, in a very small way, simply following in the footsteps of the great and the good who have gone before – like Sultan Selim II, who ordered 50,000 tulip bulbs for his garden in Constantinople.

The majority of the tulips we grow today are loud, big and beefy compared to the delicate wild species, so how was this dramatic transformation realized?

## Origin of the species

Most wild tulips originated in areas of Central Asia, the richest source of species being between the Tein-Shan and Pamir Alai mountain ranges, near Islamabad, now the capital of Pakistan. Tulips can also be found growing wild in parts of Europe such as the Balkans, Spain, Portugal, Italy and Crete, but it is thought that these must originally have been brought over by merchants and travellers coming from Central Asia and that they then escaped into the wild.

We tend to think of the original tulips as coming from Turkey, but they were also found in Russia, near the Black Sea and in the Crimea – areas that once belonged to the Turkish or Ottoman Empire. In the mid-sixteenth century European travellers brought back tales of brilliant red lilies held in high esteem by the Turks, and these are thought to have been tulips. The name tulip is said to have come from the Turkish *tuliban*, or turban – men often tucked a tulip in their turban. The first known report of a tulip growing in a western European garden was made by Conrad Gesner, a botanist who in 1559 saw tulips in a garden owned by Councillor Johannis Heinrich Herwart of Augsburg, Bavaria. The sight and scent impressed him enough for him to describe it in great detail in a book (*Caspari Collino Pharmocopoeo*) published two years later. He added that the tulips had come from seed from Constantinople.

### Turkish tulipomania

By this time the Turks were already great admirers of the tulip and in fact had been since as far back as the thirteenth century, when poets had waxed lyrical about the beauty of the flower. The Turkish word for tulip is *lale*, which uses the same letters as Allah, so the flowers were often used a religious symbol. Sultans built palaces with gardens filled with their favourite flowers, including tulips, and as the Ottoman Empire expanded, so did the style of garden. By the sixteenth century, the tulip had become a symbol of the Ottoman Empire and was to be found embroidered on robes and painted on tiles and ceramics.

By the 1630s, there were reports of many tulips being grown in gardens and offered for sale in shops. The Turks had already started, as is human nature, to organize and select the best ones, and to make official lists and rules as to what constituted a perfect bloom. They favoured narrow, pointed petals rather than the fuller, cup-shaped flowers preferred in the west. Nevertheless, there was a two-way traffic in tulips, and by the

**Left** *T. fosteriana* tulips were imported to Holland from Central Asia from 1906 onwards. The Dutch breeders valued the bright scarlet colour but the height and foliage of the species was variable so naturally occurring clones were selected. This one, Red Emperor is the best known and was widely used in tulip breeding.

time of the Tulip Era (*Lale Devri*) of 1703–1730, Sultan Ahmed III was importing vast numbers of bulbs from Holland for his gardens and for tulip festivals. Descriptions of these festivals make them sound almost decadent, and the sultan's subjects were aghast at the cost. Still more poems were penned and an illustrated book showing 49 tulips was produced around 1725. However, when Ahmed died in 1730, the impetus for tulip worship appeared to die with him.

## Dutch tulipomania

Among the first tulips to flower in Holland were those planted in August 1593 in a small garden at the University of Leiden by the head botanist, Carolus Clusius. These bulbs would have been a select collection: by this time Clusius was 67 years old, had travelled widely and had built up a network of contacts with whom he exchanged bulbs. The bulbs must have been impressive when they bloomed the following spring, because several people were interested in buying them, but Clusius refused all offers. Not surprisingly, the bulbs were stolen in the dead of night, seed from them was sown, and over a period of years, stocks were gradually built up and distributed.

Once the tulip had a foothold in western Europe it spread rapidly: botanists and merchants swapped bulbs, artists illustrated them, and the wealthy sought them as novelties and status symbols. Already they were losing the modest look of the species and were taking on a more showy appearance. Their transformation can be charted in paintings of the time.

As early as the late 1620s, a nursery trade in bulbs had been established around the town of Haarlem, where the soil proved to be ideal for tulips. The dry bulbs travel well, so it was not long before an export business had also been set up and alongside it, illustrated books were produced to show potential customers what the tulips would look like. At the same time, Amsterdam was thriving as a port and trading centre, and a

logical extension of this growth was to create an exchange there in order to handle different currencies.

All the ingredients were now in place for bulb trading to begin; add to these the tulip's unpredictable capacity to break into streaks of colour that would result in highly sought-after bulbs (see opposite page), and it is easy to see how, once increasing numbers of people started trading, a sort of madness took over. The price of the bulb would depend on its name and form but also, from 1636 onwards, the most sought-after bulbs were sold by weight (measured in *azen*) and these were traded in a tulips futures market. White tulips with breaks of red or purple were the most highly prized – some examples of the day included 'Semper Augustus' and 'Viceroy' – and the fact that such broken tulips were less vigorous and harder to increase only added to their desirability.

With more and more people dealing, a crash was inevitable and it came suddenly, early in 1637. While speculators forsook the tulip, those who loved the flower for what it was carried on buying it and growing it in their gardens.

## The French connection

Tulips were also raised in France and what was then Flanders, where many interesting varieties were bred, but these growers were not as commercially minded as the Dutch. One highly sought-after Flemish variety was 'Louis XVI', a white tulip with purple markings raised by an amateur grower in 1776. 'Mon Trésor' (1875) and 'La Reine' (1860) are two early flowering French varieties, 30–35cm (12–14in) high, that were once widely used for growing in pots. They are now nearly extinct, but 'Mon Trésor' has been specially photographed for this book (see page 8) from a private collection in Holland. Meanwhile in England, in Victorian times, tulips were also often grown in containers and their virtues were extolled by John Mollison in his book *The New Practical Window Gardener*, published in 1879.

**Right** Flaming Parrot may have the markings of an old-fashioned broken tulip but, like all such bulbs sold today, its colour breaks have occurred as a result of a genetic change not because of virus infection.

## The English tulip legacy

The tulips infected with virus that caused tulipomania are no longer sold commercially, but their descendants live on in private collections. One group that has been well documented is the English Florist tulips.

At first, English enthusiasts copied the seventeenth-century craze for broken tulips and for a time they were fashionable and a statement of wealth. However, by the early eighteenth century the chattering classes were ridiculing tulips, and the flower found more loyal champions among northern working-class artisans. These people were referred to as 'florists', meaning that they concentrated on a particular flower and made a hobby of breeding and showing it. Their living came from jobs like weaving or shoemaking, and such home-based employment meant that they were around during the day to tend their flowers. They treasured the tulips and many societies were set up in 1750–1850 to grow and show English Florist tulips. In addition, countries with Huguenot refugees, such as Ireland and Scotland, invariably started up tulip societies as well.

The English florists bred their own tulips starting with stock brought from France and Flanders, and later adding in their own seedlings. The first thing they had to do was obtain a self-coloured tulip of the right shape – a half-sphere. This was called a 'breeder'. After growing stocks

## 'Breaking' in tulips

The way a bulb from a single-coloured flower will sometimes produce a flower with two colours – one streaked and patterned over the other – has fascinated tulip lovers for centuries. Such colour breaks were considered highly desirable, but they were tantalizingly unpredictable, although there was no shortage of theories and recipes for inducing breaking. Science provided the answer in 1928, by which time viruses were beginning to be understood and more powerful microscopes were available. Dorothy Cayley, working at the then south-London-based John Innes Institute discovered that breaks could be passed from bulb to bulb. When linked to research on aphids, it was confirmed that a virus passed between tulips by aphids was responsible for the breaks.

**Below** *Tulipa turkestanica* is a species tulip with some uncharacteristic features for a tulip: there are lots of small flowers per stem and each bloom opens out to a star shape. This tulip is a modest 20cm (8in) tall but unlike many species, it multiplies quickly. The open flowers are a magnet for bees.

**Right** Mon Trésor is a historical variety introduced in France in 1875. This early-flowering tulip was once popular for growing in pots but is now only found in private collections.

of the breeder for many years, the hope was that it would break into a pattern of streaks and flecks.

The different patterns and colours had their own names: Bizarre meant the bloom was yellow with a pattern of any colour; Byloemen was a white tulip with stripes of black or purple; Rose was a white bloom with red or pink markings. There were even terms for the pattern of the markings, which are still used today: 'feathered' describes colour shading in from the edge of the petals, while a 'flame' is the markings that run from the top of the petals towards the base.

To show off their hobby, florists' feasts were regularly arranged in pubs. A meal and a competitive show of tulips would take place with the blooms displayed in brown beer bottles. However, by the 1870s the tulip had started to decline as a florists' flower – more people were now working in factories than at home, much of the land where the tulips were grown had been built on, and plants that took less time to cultivate became more popular for showing.

Today, only one of these societies remains, the Wakefield and North of England Tulip Society. It was founded in 1836 and is still active, thanks to the tireless efforts of the Akers family who have been involved for generations. The society even has its own varieties, like the red-and-white 'Wakefield', that are

passed down and preserved. There is still a show in Wakefield in May each year at which the tulips are displayed. A prize-winning tulip needs to have six even petals with clear markings that are similar on each petal. The tulips are grown under shade netting to keep them in good condition and they are picked a day or two before the show. English Florist tulips are not commercially available, but members of the society often swap surplus bulbs in autumn.

## Tulips today

Thanks to the Dutch, we now have literally thousands of varieties of tulip. Dutch interest in the flower has never ceased and they continue to be the main breeders, growers and exporters of both the bulbs and the cut flowers.

The bulb-growing regions of the Netherlands, or *bollenstreek*, are on the west coast of Holland, centred around Lisse, between the cities of Haarlem and Leiden. Here is the famous Keukenhof Garden, a shop window for the bulb industry that was established in 1949 on what were once sand dunes and beech woods. This was an enterprising move, particularly as it was created just four years after the 'hunger winter' following the Second World War, when so many Dutch starved to death. At that time, many people walked from the cities to the bulb fields to eat the bulbs. They were boiled and were said to taste sweet, a point noted by Carolus Clusius hundreds of years before. This is not a practice to be recommended as tulips are now listed as being poisonous if eaten. Today, tulips thrive on the free-draining soil at Keukenhof and the displays and planting ideas attract around 800,000 visitors a year.

To give a taste of the scale of the industry, it is estimated that the Netherlands grows at least three billion tulip bulbs each year, of which two billion are exported. The USA takes one billion and the rest go to countries such as Germany, Japan and the UK. However, there is also commercial tulip bulb growing in England on a more modest scale, centred around Spalding in Lincolnshire, where the silty soil of the Fens is ideal. Tulips are also grown in Ireland, Denmark, and Japan – farmers fit in crops of tulips between the rice harvests – as well as in Skagit Valley in Washington State, the Dandenong mountains of Australia, Tasmania and the South Island of New Zealand.

## Tulip breeding

Growing tulips as a cut flower (by 'forcing' them) is much more profitable than producing the dry bulbs for gardens, so it is this side of the business that tends to dictate which varieties are widely available. Half the Dutch-grown cut-flower tulips are made up of just ten varieties, and most breeding is concentrated on the Triumph tulips because these respond well and quickly to forcing under glass. It is therefore important for gardeners to redress the balance and choose varieties that are gardenworthy rather than merely easy for forcing, and this is where the trials and awards that assess plants on their garden merit are of such value.

Tulip breeding takes time and there are no guarantees as to the results. Only one in a thousand seedlings will have worthwhile characteristics, and it can take five to seven years for a seed to produce a flower. Bulking up enough stock to sell and market could take another 13–15 years. Because all the bulbs are clones of the original plant, once stocks are available you should be sure of what you are getting. In time the vigour of these clones can decline; this may take 40 years or so, but it depends very much on the cultivar.

All the tulips described in this book are part of a private tulip collection belonging to Cees Breed, and have been chosen because they are among the best of their type. Many of the firms who bred the tulips featured here are no longer trading as there are now fewer but larger firms.

To create new tulip cultivars, a breeder can cross two plants, collect the seed, raise the offspring and select those with interesting features. But many novel varieties – the Parrot tulips, for example – have arisen naturally from a mutation, known as a 'sport'. Sports often go on to produce more sports, so you can end up with clusters of tulips with similar characteristics in terms of height and flowering time but with a range of different colours or markings.

## Trials and awards

In the UK, the Royal Horticultural Society (RHS) has a Daffodil and Tulip Committee that gives awards to tulips for their garden performance. These are based on growing trials, visits to private collections and discussions between experts. The highest award is the Award of Garden Merit (AGM), which is given to plants that are gardenworthy and reasonably easy to grow. The AGM was re-instituted in 1992; awards given prior to this, and other awards like the Award of Merit (AM) and Highly Commended (HC), are included for historical reference only.

In Holland, the awards are organized by the Tulip Committee of the Royal General Bulb Growers' Association (KAVB). The Trial Garden Award (TGA) is worth looking out for, as it highlights varieties that perform well in the garden. Other awards include the Award of Merit (AM), the Early Forcing Award (EFA) and the First-Class Certificate (FCC).

Awards are useful when selecting tulips for the garden. They are a more impartial guide than bulb catalogues, and they point you towards gardenworthy cultivars not just those that are good as cut flowers. However, do not be too influenced by awards: your criteria may be different, or you might like a style of tulip that has not been assessed for many years. Visit gardens, particularly in your locality, and note down varieties that look good after rain or a hot spell and whose colour and form appeal to you. Try them out and note down when and how deeply you planted them, and what the display was like the following spring.

# Classification checklist

Pick up any tulip bulb catalogue and you will find the tulips grouped under headings like 'Single Early' and 'Double Late'. This is not done on the whim of the supplier, but is an internationally agreed classification organized by the KAVB (see page 9). The last register of tulip varieties and their classification was published in 1996 and listed 5,600 varieties. Its main purpose is to help people navigate their way around the 2,600 varieties that are actually available today.

Broadly speaking the classification is based on flowering season plus flower shape. There are 15 divisions: 14 cover the garden hybrids and one the species and species hybrids. Knowing which division a variety is in will help you predict when it will flower and what its characteristics will be.

**Single Early** (division one) These are the earliest tulips to flower, typically in early to mid-spring; many can also be forced to flower even earlier under glass. The bulbs can then be lifted early, so are ideal for beds where summer bedding will follow the tulips.
Apricot Beauty (see page 80)
Bellona (see page 69)
Brilliant Star (see page 76)
Charles (see page 24)
Flair (see page 25)
Generaal de Wet (see page 34)
Keizerskroon (see page 26)
Prince Carnival (see page 27)
Yokohama (see page 61)

**Double Early** (division two) Large, full blooms up to 10cm (4in) across make these tulips impressive, but some varieties are prone to flopping over unless grown in a sheltered site. They start flowering in early spring, albeit a little later than Single Early tulips; some flower in early spring others from early to mid spring.
Electra (see page 83)
Monte Carlo (see page 56)
Peach Blossom (see page 64)

Schoonoord (see page 40)
Willemsoord (see page 20)

**Triumph** (division three) These are mid-season tulips, coming into flower from mid- to late spring. The large blooms on sturdy stems make them ideal for border planting or for growing as cut flowers.
Barcelona (see page 78)
Princess Victoria (see page 84)
White Dream (see page 39)

**Darwin Hybrids** (division four) Tall tulips with large flowers, these mid-season tulips flower in mid- to late spring.
Burning Heart (see page 81)
Olympic Flame (see page 74)

**Single Late** (division five) These are also tall tulips with large flowers, which are produced in late spring. There is a wide range of different colours within this group.
Blushing Lady (see page 35)
Halcro (see page 52)
Maureen (see page 39)
Menton (see page 50)

Pink Diamond (see page 82)
Queen of Night (see page 61)
Sweet Harmony (see page 57)

**Lily-flowered** (division six) Pointed, reflexed petals give these flowers an elegant shape. Most are late-spring tulips, a few are mid-spring but all are invaluable around the garden.
Ballade (see page 17)
Elegans Alba (see page 14)
Elegant Lady (see page 79
Jacqueline (see page 18)
Queen of Sheba (see page 28)
White Triumphator (see page 23)

**Fringed** (division seven) The petals of these late-spring tulips have a fringed edge, making them very showy.
Blue Heron (see page 16)
Burgundy Lace (see page 44)
Fancy Frills (see page 85)
Hamilton (see page 58)
Maja (see page 72)

**Viridiflora** (division eight) An unusual group, the flowers have a green stripe or flame on the back of the petals. They bloom in late spring.

**Artist (see page 31)**
**Esperanto (see page 53)**
**Greenland (see page 70)**
**Spring Green (see page 71)**

**Rembrandt** (division nine) These are the blooms painted by the Dutch Old Masters (though not particularly by Rembrandt). The petals are streaked with colour caused by a virus. Strict plant health regulations mean that these particular tulips are no longer grown in the Netherlands and so cannot be obtained commercially: they are kept in existence by private collectors. Other tulips with similar markings but not caused by a virus are available.

**Parrot** (division ten) Fringed, twisted petals give these flowers the appearance of a parrot's plumage. Parrot tulips flower towards the end of spring. The stems may or may not be sturdy, depending on the variety, but in general these tulips require a sheltered site.

**Black Parrot (see page 62)**
**Blue Parrot (see page 64)**

**Estella Rijnvold (see page 42)**
**Fantasy (see page 45)**
**Flaming Parrot (see page 37)**
**Orange Favourite (see page 54)**
**Red Parrot (see page 42)**
**Texas Gold (see page 68)**
**Yellow Parrot (see page 59)**

**Double Late** (division eleven) These have large double flowers, a bit like peonies. They flower towards the end of spring and need a sheltered spot as rain can flatten them, but in the right place they have a long flowering season.

**Bonanza (see page 47)**
**Carnaval de Nice (see page 21)**
**Mount Tacoma (see page 22)**
**Uncle Tom (see page 62)**

**Kaufmanniana** (division twelve) Small tulips that flower in very early spring, these often have blooms that are bi-coloured. Some also have very attractive mottled foliage. They are ideal tulips for planting in containers, in the front of the border or for rockeries.

**Heart's Delight (see page 33)**

**Fosteriana** (division thirteen) These have similar uses to the Kaufmannianas and Greigiis, but are taller with larger flowers, so could also be used for bedding. They flower from early to mid-spring and some have attractive mottling on the foliage.

**Candela (see page 67)**
**Juan (see page 48)**
**Orange Emperor (see page 33)**
**Princeps (see page 77)**
**Purissima (see page 40)**

**Greigii** (division fourteen) The maroon mottling on the foliage is a feature of these tulips, which flower in early to mid-spring. Again, they are ideal for containers, the front of the border or rockeries.

**Cape Cod (see page 51)**
**Oratorio (see page 19)**
**Plaisir (see page 36)**
**Toronto (see page 49)**
**Yellow Dawn (see page 72)**

**Species** (division fifteen) These have not been crossed or bred but occur naturally or have been selected from natural stock. Most are low growing with star-shaped flowers, and can be left to seed and naturalize in rockeries or grass.

**Lilac Wonder (see page 66)**
**Tubergen's Gem (see page 75)**
**Fusilier (see page 46)**
**Whittallii (see page 29)**

Captions to the pictures:
1 Flair (Single Early)
2 Fancy Frills (Fringed)
3 Schoonoord (Double Early)
4 Ballade (Liliy-flowered)
5 Spring Green (Viridiflora)
6 Flaming Parrot (Parrot)
7 Burning Heart (Darwin Hybrid)
8 Princeps (Fosteriana)

# an abundance of tulips

There are thousands of tulip varieties to choose from, which is part of their attraction, but even the keenest gardener can only grow a selection in any one year. The tulips featured on the following pages come from a unique private collection in the Netherlands and provide an excellent starting point from which to explore this fascinating genus. They not only offer a visual feast but can also be relied on as being gardenworthy and among the best in their particular division. Each portrait in words highlights the attributes that make the variety special and specifies the division it belongs to. This, together with practical details like flowering height and flowering period, can be a great help when it comes to planning planting schemes. Whether you plan to grow tulips to enjoy as garden flowers or to cut and bring indoors, you are sure to find countless examples here that will fire your enthusiasm. Welcome to the world of tulipomania!

**Elegans Alba**

Group: Lily-flowered

A unique colour combination in a tulip, there is simply no other variety like this one, with its lily-flowered petals of purest ivory edged with a very narrow red rim. This historical tulip won an Award of Merit in 1895 but details of the raiser and the circumstances of its discovery are unknown. Stocks are slow to bulk up and difficult to source, so if you obtain any bulbs, you should treasure them. As a garden plant, the stems can be a little weak so it is well worth finding a sheltered site to plant this variety in. With such delicate colouring it is best to keep nearby planting subtle; violas make excellent companion plants.

**Origin:** Unknown
**Year of introduction:** Unknown
**Flowering height:** 50cm (20in)
**Flowering period:** Late spring
**Awards:** AM RHS 1895

## Blue Heron

Group: Fringed

The colour of this tulip is unique and when the flower opens, a paler inside is revealed that subtly contrasts with the darker outside. Add to this the short, crystalline fringe and you have a flower that is really special. Grow it in the garden in a spot where you can appreciate the blooms almost at eye level, or cut a few to enjoy indoors. Fringed tulips were recognized as a distinct group only in 1981, before which they were lumped together with other Single Late tulips. Blue Heron is one of the cultivars from Segers Bros, who specialized in breeding Fringed tulips.

**Breeder:** Segers Bros
**Year of introduction:** 1970
**Flowering height:** 60cm (24in)
**Flowering period:** Late spring
**Awards:** AGM RHS 1995

## Ballade

Group: Lily-flowered

The flowers of this variety are rather special, with their broad white edge. For the best blooms, plant in dappled shade or where there is sun for only part of the day, so the white edge will be protected from sun scorch. As the petals are wider and less reflexed than most Lily-flowered tulips, the blooms have more of a goblet shape. Ballade also flowers earlier than others in this group and is one of the few Lily-flowered types suitable for forcing as cut flowers. There are several sports in the pipeline that are an exciting prospect for the future: Ballade Dream (Sonnet), purple-red with a yellow base; and Ballade Orange (Je T'aime), orange with a yellow margin.

**Breeder**: Nieuwenhuis Bros
**Year of introduction**: 1953
**Flowering height**: 55cm (22in)
**Flowering period**: Mid-spring
**Awards**: AM RHS 1982, AGM RHS 1993

## Jacqueline

Group: Lily-flowered

Like all Lily-flowered tulips, Jacqueline offers both an elegant flower shape and robust weather resistance: such a combination makes this group very valuable to gardeners. The deep pink flowers look lovely underplanted with white or pink double daisies (*Bellis perennis*) or combined with a white Lily-flowered tulip like White Triumphator (see page 23). Jacqueline was bred by Segers Bros; although they are better known for their work on the Fringed tulips, they later turned their attention to improving the Lily-flowered types and this was one of the last they registered. It is tall but has very strong stems that provide good wind tolerance, making it an excellent garden tulip. Jacqueline supersedes Mariette, one of Segers Bros' first deep pink Lily-flowered tulips, registered in 1942.

**Breeder:** Segers Bros
**Year of introduction:** 1958
**Flowering height:** 70cm (28in)
**Flowering period:** Late spring
**Awards:** AM Holland 1962

## Oratorio

Group: Greigii

You will notice this little tulip as soon as its beautiful mottled leaves come through the soil. Later it will reward you with rosy-red blooms. This is one of a number of Greigii cultivars bred by the growers' co-operative Hybrida in the early 1950s; another is the more familiar scarlet Red Riding Hood. However, many find Oratorio's colour easier to place and a little more special. Its low habit makes it ideal for raised beds, rockeries, small pots and windowboxes.

**Breeder:** Hybrida
**Year of introduction:** 1953
**Flowering height:** 30cm (12in)
**Flowering period:** Early to mid-spring
**Awards:** HC RHS 1966, AM RHS 1979

### Willemsoord

Group: Double Early

This tulip is a sport of Murillo, the most important historical Double Early tulip. Murillo was introduced in 1860 by Gerard Leembruggen and has produced 140 named sports, around 20 of which are still available today. Amazingly, these were all natural mutations rather than crosses made by breeders; their wide colour range is also astonishing. Murillo sports can be grown as bedding tulips in a rainbow mixture; because they have the same parent, the flowering height and time will be the same, something that cannot be achieved with certainty with mixtures of other tulips. Willemsoord has a sport, Jan W. van Reisen, named after the person who discovered it in 1960. It is purple rather than carmine, but retains the striking white edge.

**Breeder:** Paul Roozen
**Year of introduction:** 1930
**Flowering height:** 25cm (10in)
**Flowering period:** Early spring

## Carnaval de Nice

Group: Double Late

Very eye-catching and fully double, this is just what you need to
announce the arrival of spring in a garden of dark evergreens.
Carnaval de Nice is a sport of Nizza that mutated in two ways:
the flower colour changed from red and yellow to red and white,
and the foliage sported to produce silver-edged leaves. A similar
tulip, Gerbrand Kieft, was introduced by Hybrida in 1951 and
named after one of its founders. Kieft did much to preserve and
distribute Double Late varieties when they were out of favour, so
it is apt that his namesake is one that has survived.

**Breeder:** C.G. van Tubergen
**Year of introduction:** 1953
**Flowering height:** 50cm (20in)
**Flowering period:** Late spring

## Mount Tacoma

Group: Double Late

Large bulbs of Mount Tacoma produce white flowers with attractive markings on the petals – this detail sets this variety apart from other white double tulips. Smaller bulbs are much less likely to produce the markings. Grow it in a sheltered site: a border backed with shrubs or a hedge to act as a windbreak are ideal. An alternative is to grow it in rows to use as a cut flower and to cut the stems before they snap, which can happen after a shower of rain. This is an old variety but it is still popular as it can be used to create cool calming plantings of white and green. Try it in partial shade with an underplanting of white-and-green variegated hostas and white double daisies (*Bellis perennis*).

**Breeder:** Polman-Mooy
**Year of introduction:** Before 1924
**Flowering height:** 45cm (18in)
**Flowering period:** Late spring
**Awards:** AM Holland 1926, FCC Holland 1939

## White Triumphator

Group: Lily-flowered

This tulip has staying power. Introduced in 1942, it still triumphed over rivals to receive the coveted AGM from the Royal Horticultural Society as recently as 1995 – and so has proved to be appropriately named! It stands proud on strong, sturdy stems bearing long-lasting, beautifully shaped white blooms. And as white looks good with any colour, you cannot go wrong with this popular tulip. Plant drifts of it in the middle or at the back of a border packed with lush green foliage plants, together with a white- or silver-variegated subject such as spotted-leafed pulmonaria. Or adopt a more formal approach and use it as a spring bedding plant with another late-flowering tulip or with a low underplanting.

**Breeder:** C.G. van Tubergen
**Year of introduction:** 1942
**Flowering height:** 60cm (24in)
**Flowering period:** Late spring
**Awards:** HC RHS 1982, AGM RHS 1995

## Charles

Group: Single Early

Early tulips are valued for their wide range of flower colour in early spring, but keep in mind that they will peak when the weather may be wet and windy. To improve the chances of enjoying a prolonged display, opt for robust varieties with sturdy stems, like Charles, and plant in a sheltered spot. Charles has eye-catching bright red flowers. Once open, they reveal a yellow base inside.

**Breeder:** C.P. Alkemade Junior
**Year of introduction:** 1954
**Flowering height:** 40cm (16in)
**Flowering period:** Early spring

**Flair**

Group: Single Early

A fiery little tulip whose warm hues will bring welcome colour in early to mid-spring. On close inspection, you will see that each flower is red and yellow with irregular stripes and flames. Once the flowers open, the yellow anthers stand out against the black at the base of the petals. Flair is ideal for growing in pots or other containers because its stems are fairly short. Containers also enable you to move the planting around, to a more sheltered position in bad weather or to a prominent site when the plants are in flower. To make the most of Flair's colour, try steel-grey aluminium planters or ceramic pots with a dark blue or black glaze.

**Breeder:** Jac van den Berg
**Year of introduction:** 1978
**Flowering height:** 35cm (14in)
**Flowering period:** Early spring

## Keizerskroon

Group: Single Early

Two hundred and fifty years and still growing strong, this is one of the oldest tulip cultivars, dating back to 1750, yet it was awarded a coveted AGM award from the RHS as recently as 1993. Keizerskroon (which means Emperor's Crown) is red with a broad yellow edge; in all this time it has only sported once, to create a Parrot form called Rex. Although fairly tall compared to the Greigii and Kaufmanniana hybrids, it can be grown in containers: choose deep ones such as wooden half-barrels. It combines well with wallflowers, creating a simple yet reliable cottage-garden style planting.

**Breeder:** Unknown
**Year of introduction:** 1750
**Flowering height:** 35cm (14in)
**Flowering period:** Early spring
**Awards:** AGM RHS 1993

## Prince Carnival

Group: Single Early

Like Generaal de Wet (see page 34), this tulip is a sport of the old cultivar Prince of Austria, and shares the same qualities of sweet scent and warm-coloured blooms. The flowers are red and yellow flamed. Although Prince Carnival (or Prins Carnaval) is a good garden variety, it can be hard to obtain, so keep in mind a modern alternative called Mickey Mouse, registered in 1960 by E. Kooi. It is similar in colour, but is a bit shorter at 35cm (14in) and has smaller flowers.

**Breeder:** Unknown
**Year of introduction:** 1930
**Flowering height:** 40cm (16in)
**Flowering period:** Early spring

## Queen of Sheba

Group: Lily-flowered

A truly majestic tulip prized for its glowing colour and refined lily-flowered shape. The slenderness of the young flower is emphasized by the narrowest golden-yellow edge, and as the flower matures it opens wide to reveal an unexpected greenish centre. This is an excellent garden plant from the practical point of view too, with long-lasting blooms on strong stems. So all in all, no wonder it is still winning awards nearly fifty years after it was first bred during the Second World War. Like all the lily-flowered tulips, its elegant flower profile makes an effective contrast anywhere in the garden. Use these lovely flowers to punctuate the soft hummocks of emerging perennial foliage in a border or as a focal point in a spring bedding plant display, or simply as a container plant.

**Breeder:** Dr W.E. de Mol and A.H. Nieuwenhuis
**Year of introduction:** 1944
**Flowering height:** 60cm (24in)
**Flowering period:** Late spring
**Awards:** AM RHS 1968, AGM RHS 1995

## Whittallii

Group: Species

This tulip (shown here 1½–2 times life size) is named after Ernest Whittall, a British man who lived and worked in Turkey and who discovered this species in the western part of the country while plant hunting in his spare time.

*T. whittallii* has bright bronze flowers with a touch of yellow. At first the blooms are cup shaped, then they open out into a star. Large bulbs may yield two flowers per stem. There is sometimes a variation in markings: for example, there may be a green tinge outside the flower and yellow-margined black basal marks inside, and the leaves may have red-purple margins. Close relatives include *T. orphanidea*, with orange-brown flowers, and *T. hageri*, which has flowers in a subdued red. All are similar in form, being sturdy plants that are perfect for rockeries or alpine troughs.

**Origin:** Collected by Ernest Whittall, Turkey
**Year of introduction:** Described 1929
**Flowering height:** 30cm (12in)
**Flowering period:** Mid-spring
**Awards:** AM RHS 1970

### Artist

Group: Viridiflora

A dwarf Viridiflora, with salmon petals flamed with green, this makes a good garden tulip, particularly in containers. Artist was the result of a cross between the orange Generaal de Wet (see page 34) and the Single Late red Mayflower. This early hybridizing work was undertaken by brothers Adriaan and Jan Captein of Breezand, and eventually yielded a number of other progeny. As with many intricately marked tulips, enthusiasts became obsessive about them, and for a spell in the 1950s there was a mini-tulipomania for new cultivars of Artist. One example was Hollywood, a bright red-and-green tulip that was sold for £500 per kilogram. Other sports of Artist are Golden Artist, with golden-orange petals and a green flame, and more recently Green River, which has variegated leaves of dark green and pale yellow.

**Breeder:** Captein Brothers
**Year of introduction:** 1947
**Flowering height:** 30cm (12in)
**Flowering period:** Late spring
**Awards:** AGM RHS 1995

## Orange Emperor

Group: Fosteriana

This tulip was obtained by crossing the vivid Red Emperor with a now-extinct orange Single Early tulip called Fred Moore. The result is a softer colour with a yellow centre that is much easier to place in the garden than the original Red Emperor. On close inspection of the young flowers, you will sometimes see green feathering along the midrib; although subtle, such markings are desirable features in any tulip and add to its value as a cut flower.

**Breeder:** K. van Egmond & Sons
**Year of introduction:** 1962
**Flowering height:** 40cm (16in)
**Flowering period:** Mid-spring
**Awards:** AM RHS 1979

## Heart's Delight

Group: Kaufmanniana

The short stems of the Kaufmannianas are not suitable for the lucrative cut-flower market, so little breeding work has been done on them in the past 40 years or so. This hybrid was bred in the early 1950s. The species *T. kaufmanniana* is known as the waterlily tulip, as its flowers open flat and wide in the sun like a waterlily. This characteristic is shared by others in its group. Hybrids like Heart's Delight, which have some Greigii parentage, also have attractive maroon stripes or mottling on their leaves.

**Breeder:** C.G. van Tubergen
**Year of introduction:** 1952
**Flowering height:** 20cm (8in)
**Flowering period:** Very early spring

### Generaal de Wet

Group: Single Early

This tulip was introduced a couple of years after the end of the Anglo-Boer War (1899–1902) and so was named after farmer-turned-war-hero Generaal Christiaan Rudolph de Wet. The first orange sport of Prince of Austria, an orange-scarlet scented tulip dating back to 1860, it has a long and noble pedigree. Not many cultivars scoop an RHS Award of Merit in the year they are introduced; fewer still are going strong nearly 100 years later. Its unique colouring – yellow-orange with delicate orange-red stippling – plus its very sweet scent make it still worth growing today. Plant outdoors for early colour in beds and borders, or indoors as a forced tulip.

**Breeder:** Unknown
**Year of introduction:** 1904
**Flowering height:** 40cm (16in)
**Flowering period:** Early spring
**Awards:** AM RHS 1904

**Blushing Lady**

Group: Single Late

This tulip is one of the newest in a long line of Single Late varieties bred by D.W. Lefeber & Co. At first, Mariette, a Lily-flowered tulip, was crossed with a Greigii and the result was the warm salmon-pink-red Temple of Beauty (1959), with pointed petals and slightly mottled young leaves. Temple of Beauty proved to be a useful cut flower, and produced many sports including Blushing Beauty (1983), with flowers of soft orange with red flames and a yellow centre. Blushing Beauty produced a more intensely coloured sport in Blushing Lady which, like Temple of Beauty, has very tall stems and rather elongated flowers that are long lasting.

**Breeder:** D.W. Lefeber & Co and J.N.M. van Eeden
**Year of introduction:** 1991
**Flowering height:** 75cm (30in)
**Flowering period:** Late spring

## Plaisir

Group: Greigii

Most Greigii hybrids are gardenworthy, but Plaisir is one of the best. It is ideal for small gardens, windowboxes, balconies and patios. When the flowers first appear they have an elegant pointed shape; as they mature, you notice the feathered markings and the contrast of the dark centre. An interesting variation on Plaisir is its sport Californian Sun, yellow with a large scarlet flame, registered by J. Prins & Sons in 1988.

**Breeder:** Hybrida
**Year of introduction:** 1953
**Flowering height:** 25cm (10in)
**Flowering period:** Early to mid-spring
**Awards:** AM RHS 1979, AGM RHS 1993

## Flaming Parrot

Group: Parrot

In Japan, this particular variety, with its subtle coloration and beautiful form, is highly sought after for cut-flower arrangements. It has the appearance of an old Rembrandt tulip but the markings are due to a natural mutation rather than a virus. This extrovert Parrot tulip arose as a sport of Red Parrot (see page 42); the only difference between the two is the colour. In all other respects – such as sturdy stems and flowering time – they are the same.

**Breeder:** P. Heemskerk
**Year of introduction:** 1968
**Flowering height:** 70cm (28in)
**Flowering period:** Late spring
**Awards:** TGA Holland 1968

## Maureen

Group: Single Late

One of the tallest tulips, its long, strong stems are topped with egg-shaped, marble-white blooms. It is a white seedling of Mrs John T. Scheepers, another Single Late tulip with egg-shaped blooms. Maureen is very tolerant of warm conditions and so is popular in southern states of the USA, where most tulips would flag in the heat. Commercial growers in the South of France grow it as a cut flower for Paris markets, because they can get it in bloom a fortnight earlier than rival growers in Holland. The recent AGM from the RHS will reassure gardeners in the UK that Maureen still has plenty to offer as a garden variety although it is expensive compared to most tulips.

**Breeder:** Segers Bros
**Year of introduction:** 1950
**Flowering height:** 70cm (28in)
**Flowering period:** Late spring
**Awards:** AM RHS 1960, AGM RHS 1993

## White Dream

Group: Triumph

The Triumph group was developed from the early twentieth century onwards to meet the demand for tulips for the popular bedding displays in public parks. Such tulips needed to be uniform, like soldiers on parade, with little variation in height or flowering time and with sturdy stems so that there would be no slouching in the ranks. White Dream has charming flowers, although they are smaller than is typical for a Triumph tulip, and it is a reliable choice for beds or large tubs.

**Breeder:** J.F. van den Berg & Sons
**Year of introduction:** 1972
**Flowering height:** 50cm (20in)
**Flowering period:** Mid-spring

## Purissima

Group: Fosteriana

The only white-flowered member of the Fosteriana group, Purissima (sometimes sold as White Emperor) is adored for its large, bowl-shaped blooms, ably supported against adverse weather by sturdy grey-green stems and foliage. The yellow at the base of the petals is a hint that it might produce yellow sports, as it did with Yellow Purissima (1980) and more recently Purissima King (1994) – red with a yellow base.

**Breeder:** C.G. van Tubergen
**Year of introduction:** 1943
**Flowering height:** 45cm (18in)
**Flowering period:** Early spring
**Awards:** AM Holland 1949

## Schoonoord

Group: Double early

A white sport of the important Murillo (see Willemsoord, page 20), its discoverer and date of discovery are unknown, although it won an award in 1909. Its white colour means that Schoonoord will mix beautifully with any of the other Murillo sports, while its short stems also make it a neat candidate for pots and windowboxes: you could try it in combination with blue grape hyacinths (*Muscari*) for a cool, refreshing planting.

**Breeder:** Unknown
**Year of introduction:** Unknown
**Flowering height:** 25cm (10in)
**Flowering period:** Early spring
**Awards:** FCC Holland 1909

## Estella Rijnveld

Group: Parrot

The blooms of this variety are like generous scoops of raspberry ripple ice-cream. Its alternative name, Gay Presto, sums up its exuberance. With characteristic feathered plumage, Estella Rijnveld arose as a mutation of Cordell Hull, a Single Late tulip with red flowers and white flames. Tulip aficionados value Estella Rijnveld for her plentiful feathers. The stems are shorter than a typical Parrot tulip, which makes for a sturdy plant, ideal for containers or an open border.

**Breeder:** Segers Bros
**Year of introduction:** 1954
**Flowering height:** 50cm (20in)
**Flowering period:** Late spring

## Red Parrot

Group: Parrot

Parrot tulips are some of the showiest and there is always great demand for them. As a result, they are rather expensive and supplies can be limited. But even a handful, with their large fringed and ruffled blooms, will pack a punch. Strong colours abound and Red Parrot, with its very intense red coloration, is a perfect example. Flower arrangers adore Parrot tulips – apart from the pollen that stains – but they are excellent garden plants too. Red Parrot has long stems but they are strong and can withstand bad weather if planted in a sheltered site.

**Breeder:** J.C. Evers
**Year of introduction:** 1940
**Flowering height:** 70cm (28in)
**Flowering period:** Late spring

**Burgundy Lace**

Group: Fringed

This is one of the last of the Fringed tulips to come into flower, so is a useful insurance if you live in an area with cold springs. The tall stems bear carmine-red blooms, which make it an ideal companion to the yellow-flowered Maja (see page 72) which has a similar habit and flowering time. Introduced in 1961, Burgundy Lace was one of the early crosses made by Segers Bros; the uniform colour was much in demand in the 1970s and 1980s, and it is still popular today as it is a good perennial tulip.

**Breeder:** Segers Bros
**Year of introduction:** 1961
**Flowering height:** 70cm (28in)
**Flowering period:** Late spring
**Awards:** AM RHS 1970

### Fantasy

Group: Parrot

This is one of the oldest Parrot tulips, but is still very popular and is a great favourite with flower arrangers. Compared to modern Parrot tulips, the stems are rather weak, so it needs a sheltered position to achieve an upright display. Alternatively, use the lax stems to your advantage: grow it in a large hanging basket so that when the flowers droop down you can look up to admire them. Fantasy arose as a sport of a salmon-pink tulip called Clara Butt, at one time a very popular cultivar of the Darwin group. This group no longer exists and has been consolidated into the Single Late group.

**Breeder:** Unknown
**Year of introduction:** 1910
**Flowering height:** 55cm (22in)
**Flowering period:** Late spring
**Awards:** AM RHS 1921, AGM RHS 1993

## Fusilier

Group: Species

The species *T. praestans*, a native of Central Asia, is rarely grown as this particular cultivar selected by Jac Roozen has so much more to offer. Fusilier has not one but up to six flowers per stem and the blooms are an almost unbelievably bright colour. This incredible flowering impact in a very small space is invaluable to anyone who is short of planting room – you could easily tuck a row of Fusilier in the front of a narrow or packed bed. It is also a very easy tulip to grow; while many of the smaller species bulbs are rather tricky, this one has larger, tougher bulbs and once planted it will be long lived. For an even more colourful effect, you could plant the sport, *T. praestans* 'Unicum', which has a pale yellow rim around each leaf.

**Breeder:** Jac B. Roozen
**Year of introduction:** Unknown
**Flowering height:** 35cm (14in)
**Flowering period:** Early spring
**Awards:** AM RHS 1966

## Bonanza

Group: Double Late

As its name suggests, this tulip delivers something extra: really full double blooms that flower for a long period by tulip standards. Fortunately, the heavy flowers are well supported by strong stems, a characteristic that makes it a good choice for forcing. The warm colours of orange-red with a yellow edge ensure this is a welcome spring flower. If you cannot find supplies, a suitable substitute is Allegretto, another Double Late tulip whose flowers are also red with a yellow edge, but it is slightly shorter at 35cm (14in).

**Breeder:** Unknown
**Year of introduction:** 1943
**Flowering height:** 40cm (16in)
**Flowering period:** Late spring
**Awards:** AM Holland 1943

### Juan

Group: Fosteriana

The species *T. fosteriana* was discovered in what is now Tajikistan and Uzbekistan, and arrived in Holland around 1906. Dutch growers were attracted by the vivid red colour and long flowers, and it proved to be a good breeding plant. Many hybrids were introduced from the 1940s to the 1970s, including Juan. The eye-catching combination of deep orange blooms with prominent yellow bases is unique; put this together with the maroon stripes on the foliage and you have a tulip that is colourful enough to be grown in a bed on its own.

**Breeder:** C.G. van Tubergen
**Year of introduction:** 1961
**Flowering height:** 45cm (18in)
**Flowering period:** Early spring

## Toronto

Group: Greigii

These warm coloured blooms nestling in their lightly speckled foliage offer easy and reliable colour. Toronto is a typical Greigii tulip but with the bonus that it is sometimes multiflowered, which means it can produce more than one flower per stem. Tuck these bulbs into the smallest of spaces, at the front of mature shrubs or in small pots or windowboxes, and you will be sure of plenty of impact. At close quarters, the open flower reveals yellow at the base of the petals, overlaid with bronze. This hint of other colours lurking just below the surface has resulted in two interesting multiflowered sports: first, Orange Toronto (1987) – like its parent save for its marigold-orange colour – and more recently Quebec (1991) – a scarlet sport with green margins on its petals and a yellow base.

**Breeder:** Jac Uittenbogaard & Sons
**Year of introduction:** 1963
**Flowering height:** 35cm (14in)
**Flowering period:** Early to mid-spring
**Awards:** AGM RHS 1993

## Menton

Group: Single Late

This is tall and sturdy with a very big egg-shaped flower. It has deep pink petals with an orange flush and is one of several sports produced by Renown, a rose-red tulip with large flowers that, in turn, originated as a seedling from Mrs John T. Scheepers. Menton is a city on the French Riviera renowned for its gardens and flower displays. Here citrus trees, palms and mimosa thrive in the sunny, subtropical climate, and so too does the heat-tolerant tulip named after it. Likewise, it is a suitable for the warmth of the southern states of the USA.

**Breeder:** W. Dekker & Sons
**Year of introduction:** 1971
**Flowering height:** 65cm (26in)
**Flowering period:** Late spring

## Cape Cod

Group: Greigii

Named after Cape Cod, near Boston, this particular Greigii tulip is popular in the USA. Like the other Greigii tulips bred by Hybrida in the 1950s, it has attractive mottled foliage and a neat habit, so is excellent for providing pockets of early colour in small spaces. What makes this one different from its red-flowered relatives is its colour; from a distance, the flowers give the impression of an apricot-coloured haze, but close up you can see that they have red outer petals with yellow edges, while inside they are yellow with a feathered red stripe.

**Breeder:** Hybrida
**Year of introduction:** 1955
**Flowering height:** 30cm (12in)
**Flowering period:** Early to mid-spring

## Halcro

Group: Single Late

A very tall tulip that is also one of the last to come into flower, its long-lasting blooms can still be showing colour into early summer in Holland, if the weather is not too warm. Plant the bulbs in drifts in the middle or at the back of a herbaceous border, and wait for the egg-shaped, carmine-red blooms to add their structure and vibrant colour to the emerging green foliage. With such long-lasting blooms, Halcro also makes a reliable cut flower.

**Breeder:** Segers Bros
**Year of introduction:** 1949
**Flowering height:** 70cm (28in)
**Flowering period:** Late spring
**Awards:** AM RHS 1977

## Esperanto

Group: Viridiflora

This tulip has the same dwarf habit as Artist but its flowers are red with green markings. The silver-white variegated leaves make it an interesting subject for growing in containers; an underplanting of white violas would echo its colouring. Esperanto is a sport of Hollywood, which in turn is a sport of Artist (see page 31).

**Breeder:** J. Pranger
**Year of introduction:** 1968
**Flowering height:** 30cm (12in)
**Flowering period:** Late spring
**Awards:** TGA Holland 1977

**Orange Favourite**

Group: Parrot

Here is one of the most fragrant tulips, yet there is plenty of visual interest as well, with the lovely orange flowers lightly streaked with green feathers. Like most Parrot tulips, Orange Favourite becomes more exciting as the blooms open and the symmetry gives way to a wild exotic look – in this particular variety, the petals open to show a prominent yellow centre. The stems can be rather lax, allowing the blooms to flop, so take this into account when deciding where to grow them – a container placed where you can look up at the open flowers is ideal. Grey, white or black containers would make a good contrast: terrazzo (available in white or grey), painted wood or fibreglass (available in many finishes) are also all worth considering.

**Breeder:** K.C. Vooren
**Year of introduction:** 1930
**Flowering height:** 50cm (20in)
**Flowering period:** Late spring
**Awards:** HC RHS 1982

## Monte Carlo

Group: Double Early

A good bet, this money-spinning tulip occupies the largest hectarage in Holland and commercial growers force millions of bulbs every year to produce cut flowers. Monte Carlo is also excellent in the garden, as confirmed by its AGM from the RHS. Plant it in a raised bed or in pots and tubs to create splashes of spring cheer, or try forcing a batch as you would prepared hyacinths and enjoy their fragrance indoors. There is one sport, called Monsella (1981), which is yellow with a red flame; the markings are variable, and even on Monte Carlo there is sometimes the merest hint of red.

**Breeder:** Anton Nijssen & Sons
**Year of introduction:** 1955
**Flowering height:** 30cm (12in)
**Flowering period:** Early spring
**Awards:** AGM RHS 1993

### Sweet Harmony

Group: Single Late

Dutch growers have a nickname
for this tulip – eggnog with cream
(*advocaat met slagroom*) – which
describes its lovely colour very
well. Although now quite an old
tulip, it is still popular in many
countries for the combination of
pale yellow with an ivory-white
edge. Sweet Harmony would look
wonderful alongside another
Single Late tulip, Blue Aimable,
with its lavender-mauve flowers.
The strong stems, shorter than
most Single Late tulips, make this
a useful tulip for planting in tubs.

**Breeder:** Jac B. Roozen
**Year of introduction:** 1944
**Flowering height:** 45-50cm (18-20in)
**Flowering period:** Late spring
**Awards:** AM RHS 1955, AGM RHS
1993

## Hamilton

Group: Fringed

This tall, elegant tulip was one of the last to be registered by Segers Bros. Its deep yellow flowers exhibit the classic crisp fringe along the edge of the petals that is the characteristic of the Fringed group. Its flowers are particularly long lasting and are worth placing where you can look at them at close quarters and marvel at the delicate serration. An alternative is to grow a row, perhaps in the vegetable patch or another area of spare ground, and use them as a source of cut flowers for the house. At one time Hamilton was used commercially as a forcing tulip, but it fell from favour as it was susceptible to a virus; however, the present stock is now clean so it makes a good garden plant.

**Breeder:** Segers Bros
**Year of introduction:** 1974
**Flowering height:** 65cm (26in)
**Flowering period:** Late spring
**Awards:** AGM RHS 1995

### Yellow Parrot

Group: Parrot

Here we see a Parrot tulip opened out to full extent, with its ruffle-edged petals almost waving like flags in the wind. In contrast, when the flower first emerges, it looks quite sedate and this change in form as the bloom matures goes some way to explaining why gardeners and flower arrangers alike find the Parrots so fascinating. Members of this group are simply sports of ordinary tulips; they were first mentioned in 1660 and the French called them Monstreuses. Most arise spontaneously, but breeders can also create Parrots either by hybridizing or by using radiation. Yellow Parrot was introduced in 1973, so it is relatively new. Like many of the more recent Parrots, it has very strong stems that support the full blooms well, making it a good garden variety – hence its Dutch Trial Garden Award.

**Breeder:** C. van Dijk
**Year of introduction:** 1973
**Flowering height:** 55cm (22in)
**Flowering period:** Late spring
**Awards:** TGA Holland 1973

## Yokohama

Group: Single Early

This golden-yellow tulip is especially renowned for its long-lasting blooms, a useful characteristic for both a garden plant and a cut flower, as tulip flowers are generally rather fleeting. Note also the elongated petals with their pointed tips, a shape that makes for an elegant and refined bloom. Yokohama is named after the Japanese city of the same name. This variety is suitable for forcing.

**Breeder:** J.F. van den Berg & Sons
**Year of introduction:** 1961
**Flowering height:** 35cm (14in)
**Flowering period:** Early spring

## Queen of Night

Group: Single Late

An outstanding tulip and the nearest we have to a black, this one is special yet easy and reliable. You could plant a group in front of silver-leafed perennials, pair it with the perennial wallflower *Erysimum* 'Bowles' Mauve' or team it with white, pink or red Single Late tulips. A recent sport is the double-flowered Black Hero, registered by J. Beerepoot in 1984: stocks are only just becoming available but it sounds exciting.

**Breeder:** J.J. Grullemans & Sons
**Year of introduction:** 1944
**Flowering height:** 60cm (24in)
**Flowering period:** Late spring
**Awards:** AM Holland 1944

### Uncle Tom

Group: Double Late

This cultivar is the deepest red of the Double Late tulips and is enjoying a revival, as garden designers encourage us to be bolder with our colour schemes and there is more interest in forcing double tulips. Like all peony-flowered varieties, a spell of dry weather is required while they are flowering otherwise the stems may not support the full blooms. Alternatively, grow them in rows as cut flowers and pick them just as they are opening. For the same shape of flower in an unusual silver-pink, go for the more widely available Angélique.

**Breeder**: Zocher & Co.
**Year of introduction**: around 1935–1939
**Flowering height**: 45cm (18in)
**Flowering period**: Late spring
**Awards**: AM Holland 1939

### Black Parrot

Group: Parrot

The black-maroon flower makes this a highly desirable Parrot tulip. Its stems are stiff enough to make it a successful spring bedding plant and it would combine well with yellow or orange wallflowers. When growing it as a container plant, choose a silver- or grey-coloured container – either a metal planter or a metallic-glazed pot. Plant where you can enjoy it at fairly close quarters. This tulip emerged as a sport of a very old Single Late tulip called Philippe de Comines (1891), which has a small maroon-black flower.

**Breeder**: C. Keur & Sons
**Year of introduction**: 1937
**Flowering height**: 50cm (20in)
**Flowering period**: Late spring
**Awards**: AGM RHS 1995

## Peach Blossom

Group: Double Early

Peach Blossom was one of the first sports of the important historical tulip Murillo (see Willemsoord, page 20) and, with its deep rose-pink peony-like flowers, is still the most popular. The flowers are borne on short stems, making them ideal for small pots or even windowboxes, particularly if underplanted with golden-leafed feverfew (*Tanacetum parthenium* 'Aureum'). Since its introduction, Peach Blossom has produced several sports – Garanza, deep peach-blossom pink; Robert Spencer, deep rose and Willem van Oranje, orange-flushed copper-red.

**Breeder:** Unknown
**Year of introduction:** 1890
**Flowering height:** 25cm (10in)
**Flowering period:** Early spring
**Awards:** AM Holland 1913

## Blue Parrot

Group: Parrot

The only violet Parrot tulip now in commercial cultivation, this was found as a mutation in a stock of Bleu Aimable, a Single Late tulip. It was registered by J.F. Charles Dix, who was legendary for his work on many tulip groups and for his longevity – he died aged 106. Its large flowers are supported by stiff, upright stems, making it very gardenworthy. As the flowers open, the ruffled petals curve outwards to reveal a dark centre against the pale stigma.

**Breeder:** J.F. Charles Dix
**Year of introduction:** 1935
**Flowering height:** 55cm (22in)
**Flowering period:** Late spring
**Awards:** AM Holland

## Lilac Wonder

Group: Species

No wonder this little tulip (shown here 1½ times life size) is a best seller: anyone who sees the combination of intense lilac and egg-yolk yellow on the small, star-like flowers and the waxy shine of its leaves will be enticed into buying. Lilac Wonder is a cultivar of the smaller, rather less showy *T. bakeri*, although it resembles another species, *T. saxatilis*, which has led to some confusion over its full name. UK taxonomists refer to it as *T. saxatilis* Bakeri Group 'Lilac Wonder' and it is often described and sold as *T. saxatilis* 'Lilac Wonder' – however, the Dutch registration committee believes it is closer genetically to *T. bakeri*. To be sure of plenty of flowers, it is vital to plant it in a warm, dry spot, perhaps in a rockery or at the foot of a sun-baked wall. If you have any gaps between paving slabs, these too could be a perfect site for Lilac Wonder: it spreads a little via stolons (spreading stems with roots) but not much.

**Breeder:** Kees Visser
**Year of introduction:** 1971
**Flowering height:** 15cm (6in)
**Flowering period:** Late spring
**Awards:** AGM RHS 1995

## Candela

Group: Fosteriana

Candela is a good example of the plant breeder's magic. Its parent was the brilliant scarlet *T. fosteriana*, yet by crossing this species with its long flowers with Single Early tulips, the breeders created varieties with their own character – they had the flower shape and flowering time of the species but with an increased colour range. Candela is a prime example of such a cross; its almost oblong flowers are a pure buttercup-yellow, yet they appear slightly later than the Single Early tulips. Once open, the flowers reveal their black anthers – a sharp contrast with the yellow. This is a variety you can rely on to emerge year after year, so it is a good choice for a low-maintenance border.

**Breeder:** K. van Egmond & Sons
**Year of introduction:** 1961
**Flowering height:** 35cm (14in)
**Flowering period:** Mid-spring
**Awards:** TGA Holland 1961

### Texas Gold

Group: Parrot

Texas Gold is one of the latest-flowering tulips: fortunately it can withstand the higher temperatures that can occur in late spring. The yellow flowers have green markings initially, but in time they have a very narrow red edge. As with some other Parrot tulips (see Orange Favourite, page 54), the stems tend to curve, so try to position them where they can be viewed from below. In 1958 J.J. de Wit found and registered a red-flamed sport of Texas Gold, which he named Texas Flame.

**Breeder:** G. van den Meij & Sons
**Year of introduction:** 1944
**Flowering height:** 45cm (18in)
**Flowering period:** Late spring

## Bellona

Group: Single Early

The very sweet scent of this tulip marks it out as something special. To best appreciate its fragrance and to protect the blooms from bad weather, grow a batch of Bellona indoors, forcing them as you would prepared hyacinths: then you will be able to enjoy their scented flowers in late winter. Alternatively, plant outside in the usual way but choose a warm sheltered position as this will not only protect the early blooms from wind but will bring out and retain the scent. A row of these golden-yellow flowers would look stunning underplanted with a carpet of blue or purple violas or pansies. Bellona is a sport from an old orange-red tulip called Prince of Austria (see Generaal de Wet, page 34) that dates back to 1860.

**Breeder:** H. de Graaf & Sons
**Year of introduction:** 1944
**Flowering height:** 50cm (20in)
**Flowering period:** Early spring

## Greenland

Group: Viridiflora

Viridiflora is derived from the Latin *viridi* meaning 'green' and flora meaning 'flower'. The appeal of this tulip is that the green appears as an elegant flame running up the middle of the petals rather than covering the whole bloom, which would be no fun at all. These tulips were only given their own group in 1987, before which they were classified by flowering time. Greenland (or, more correctly, Groenland) has a strong stem and is the largest of the group. It has produced a recent sport called New Wave, that is a Parrot version of the parent.

**Breeder:** J.F. van den Berg & Sons
**Year of introduction:** 1955
**Flowering height:** 55cm (22in)
**Flowering period:** Late spring
**Awards:** AM Holland 1960

## Spring Green

Group: Viridiflora

For many discerning gardeners, including Christopher Lloyd of the famous Great Dixter garden in Sussex, this is the best Viridiflora. The cool combination of green flame and white edge seems very contemporary and it is easy to imagine it arising out of clumps of bold foliage plants like hostas and ferns, yet Spring Green was actually introduced in the psychedelic 1960s. As one of the taller Viridifloras, it can be used to good effect in the middle and at the back of borders or in beds with an underplanting. If you can spare any, try cutting the flowers to enjoy them indoors.

**Breeder:** P. Liefting
**Year of introduction:** 1969
**Flowering height:** 50cm (20in)
**Flowering period:** Late spring
**Awards:** AGM RHS 1993

## Maja

Group: Fringed

This close-up of Maja shows the intricacy of the serration that makes the Fringed tulips so fascinating. They are a subtle version of Parrot tulips, which also arose originally as natural sports. In 1925 a red Darwin tulip called Orion sported fringed petals – it was named Sundew, presumably after the insectivorous plant that has a fringe of hairs with which to trap insects. More Fringed tulips then occurred, including some whose spiky edges were in a contrasting colour. Rather than leave the emergence of new Fringed tulips to chance, in the 1960s and 1970s breeders took matters into their own hands. Maja is one of the results. Its late-flowering primrose-coloured blooms are a particularly attractive shade of yellow and the plants are very sturdy growers.

**Breeder:** Segers Bros
**Year of introduction:** 1968
**Flowering height:** 65cm (26in)
**Flowering period:** Late spring

## Yellow Dawn

Group: Greigii

These flowers, with their sunrise colours, are stunning and as they age they open out like stars. Yellow Dawn has many practical attributes as well: its stocky habit and sturdy growth makes it an easy subject for rockeries, containers and windy gardens. To bring spring interest to a border or rose garden, plant these tulips at the front so that their maroon-mottled foliage will frame the edge. As the flowers come back reliably year after year, they are invaluable for low-maintenance planting schemes.

**Breeder:** Hybrida
**Year of introduction:** 1953
**Flowering height:** 35cm (14in)
**Flowering period:** Early to mid-spring
**Awards:** HC RHS 1966

## Olympic Flame

Group: Darwin Hybrid

Aptly named, this tulip looks like a flaming torch with its red markings on yellow petals. This is both an excellent garden variety and cut flower, as the stems are strong and sturdy and the flowers are scented. Although this particular tulip was introduced by A. Verschoor, it is a sport of Lefeber's Favourite – and Dirk Lefeber deserves a mention, as it was largely his work of crossing the Fosterianas with the Darwin tulips that created the Darwin Hybrids in the first place. These include a couple of other tulips like Oxford and Parade that are similar to Olympic Flame but taller. Today, Darwin Hybrids are the second most widely grown type of tulip in Holland, second only to the Triumph tulips which are easier to force.

**Breeder:** A. Verschoor Jr
**Year of introduction:** 1971
**Flowering height:** 55cm (22in)
**Flowering period:** Mid-spring

## Tubergen's Gem

Group: Species

What a delight to watch the change in colour as these graceful blooms open and unfurl. At first the closed flowers are red with just the hint of a yellow edge; then, as their petals partly open, the yellow of the inside is revealed. The species (*T. clusiana* var. *chrysantha*, to give it its full botanical name) is often shy to flower, but Tubergen's Gem is larger and this increased size means it produces bigger bulbs with more reserves, which increases the reliability of flowering. Even so, this is a small tulip, so plant it where it will not be smothered by neighbouring plants. A warm, dry place like a rockery, gravel garden or alpine trough would suit it best.

**Breeder:** C.G. van Tubergen
**Year of introduction:** 1969
**Flowering height:** 25cm (10in)
**Flowering period:** Early to mid-spring
**Awards:** TGA Holland 1971

## Brilliant Star

Group: Single Early

Brilliant Star is also known by the Dutch as the Christmas Tulip because it can be forced into flower at this time. A historical tulip, whose raiser is unknown, it is still available and is especially popular in Scandinavia as it performs well in poor light. It is also used by breeders to pass on its fiery red colour to other taller-stemmed tulips. There are two sports to look out for – Joffre (1931), yellow with red markings and only 13cm (5in) tall – and Sint Maarten (1983), deep orange with red flames, 30cm (12in) tall.

**Breeder:** Unknown
**Year of introduction:** 1906
**Flowering height:** 30cm (12in)
**Flowering period:** Early spring
**Awards:** FCC Holland 1908

## Princeps

Group: Fosteriana

One of the easiest ways to grow tulips, particularly if your soil is wet and sticky or just difficult, is to plant them in containers. This sturdy tulip, with its short stems topped with red flowers, is perfect for small pots, windowboxes or windy gardens. Princeps is a clone that was selected by Jan Roes from a batch of *T. fosteriana* bulbs imported from Central Asia, and is of particular interest to breeders as it retains the species' resistance to tulip-breaking virus.

**Breeder:** Jan Roes
**Year of introduction:** Unknown
**Flowering height:** 25cm (10in)
**Flowering period:** Early spring

**Barcelona**

Group: Triumph

One of the most outstanding of the newer Triumph tulips, Barcelona is predicted to be a best seller thanks to its intense colour and strong stems. The blooms start off egg-shaped rather than the conical shape normally associated with Triumph tulips, and then open out as they mature. Barcelona is very similar to the well-known Attila, a popular tulip since its introduction in 1945, the main difference being that Barcelona is slightly pinker and a bit taller. As the stocks of Attila start to weaken and become less vigorous, Barcelona is in line to replace it.

**Breeder:** Hybris
**Year of introduction:** 1989
**Flowering height:** 60cm (24in)
**Flowering period:** Mid-spring

## Elegant Lady

Group: Lily-flowered

Creamy yellow overlaid with a warm pink flush, this tulip has a colouring that is exquisite so make sure you grow it in a spot where you can linger and appreciate it. Elegant Lady was registered by Niewenhuis Bros of Lisse, a nursery that, from the 1930s to the 1960s, was a prominent breeder of many excellent Lily-flowered tulips including Ballade, Queen of Sheba, Maytime and West Point. Lily-flowered tulips make stalwart garden plants; flowering in late spring, they often escape the worst of the weather. Their pointed and reflexed petals make a graceful silhouette that then opens out in warm weather.

**Breeder:** Nieuwenhuis Bros
**Year of introduction:** 1953
**Flowering height:** 60cm (24in)
**Flowering period:** Late spring

### Apricot Beauty

Group: Single Early

The colour of this early season tulip is delicate yet breathtaking – the colour changes as the flower ages, and as it opens up, the inside is revealed to be richer than the outside. Even the best photograph rarely does justice to the texture and colour. There are few pastel shades in early spring, so this flower offers a real alternative to the usual run of brighter colours. Plant up several pots of this variety and position them on the patio, where you can enjoy their blooms and wavy leaves – it combines well with white tulips like Diana or White Hawk. Apricot Beauty can be forced indoors as you would prepared hyacinths, and will then flower in late winter. Bestseller, with copper-orange flowers, is a lesser-known sport of Apricot Beauty.

**Breeder:** C. Vlugt van Kimmenade
**Year of introduction:** 1953
**Flowering height:** 45cm (18in)
**Flowering period:** Early spring
**Awards:** EFA Holland 1961

## Burning Heart

Group: Darwin Hybrid

A gorgeous colour combination, this has an ivory-cream flower with a delicate flame of pink-red. Peer inside the open bloom and the flame markings are brighter still. Burning Heart is a recent sport of Ivory Floradale, an ivory-cream tulip with small amounts of red spotting; this in turn is a sport of a red tulip called Floradale. Like most Darwin Hybrids, Burning Heart has large flowers on strong, sturdy stems that make it a most lovely cut flower.

**Breeder:** J.N.M. van Eeden
**Year of introduction:** 1991
**Flowering height:** 55cm (22in)
**Flowering period:** Mid-spring
**Awards:** TGA Holland 1991

## Pink Diamond

Group: Single Late

When this clear but soft pink colour was first introduced it was so much in demand by the Japanese that bulbs were very expensive. Now, although it is still popular in Japan, prices are on a par with other special tulips and it costs no more than say, Queen of Night (see page 61), making it a candidate for bedding as well as containers. When you study the flowers close up, you can see that the edges of the outside petals are a lighter pink, and once the blooms are open, a grey-yellow centre can be seen. When using this tulip in colour schemes, try to combine it with white, cream or pale blue flowers.

**Breeder:** C.N. Verbruggen
**Year of introduction:** 1976
**Flowering height:** 50cm (20in)
**Flowering period:** Late spring
**Awards:** TGA Holland 1976

## Electra

Group: Double Early

It is easy to mistake this lovely tulip for a peony, yet it is much more versatile. With its short, sturdy stems, it can be grown in containers, either outdoors or forced under cover, or it can be used in a mixture of bedding tulips of Murillo sports. For an eye-catching spring bedding scheme, combine it with the white Schoonoord (see page 40); if you cannot obtain Electra, use its sport Willemsoord (see page 20) instead.

**Breeder:** Unknown
**Year of introduction:** 1905
**Flowering height:** 25cm (10in)
**Flowering period:** Early spring
**Awards:** FCC Holland 1912, 1995

## Princess Victoria

Group: Triumph

White and carmine almost blend together to produce the soft, feminine coloration in this flower. As is typical of the (relatively) more recent Triumph tulips, Princess Victoria has a sturdy habit and is a good forcing tulip. Los Angeles – apricot-red flowers with a yellow edge – is another variety with blended colours introduced by the same breeder.

**Breeder:** J.F. van den Berg & Sons
**Year of introduction:** 1979
**Flowering height:** 50cm (20in)
**Flowering period:** Mid- to late spring
**Awards:** AGM RHS 1995

## Fancy Frills

Group: Fringed

Fringed tulips arose as sports between 1925 and 1930 (see Maja, page 72), but in the 1960s and early 1970s Segers Bros, among others, created more by hybridizing Fringed sports with Single Late tulips. Through crosses with Triumphs, they also bred Fringed tulips that could be forced as cut flowers. Fancy Frills is one of the earliest Fringed tulips to come into flower, ideal for a patio planter and one of the very few in this group that is suitable for forcing. It shows the characteristic serrations on the edges of the petals, plus it has an attractive rose-pink flower with a white base. Segers Bros closed in 1975, only three years after this lovely tulip was released, and the stock was transferred to a W.A.M. Pennings.

**Breeder:** Segers Bros (registered with W.A.M. Pennings)
**Year of introduction:** 1972
**Flowering height:** 45cm (18in)
**Flowering period:** Late spring
**Awards:** AGM RHS 1995

# tulips in the garden

Tulips are easy to grow if you follow three basic principles: always buy top-quality bulbs, choose the right position for them and plant them correctly. You can treat them either as annuals or perennials, but with care, almost all tulips will flower for many years.

Their brief flowering season can be shortened by bad weather, so in a cold or exposed garden, concentrate on mid- to late-season tulips and in a warm climate, put the emphasis on the early flowerers. You could even plant an early and a late tulip in the same planting hole or plant several layers of bulbs, as has been done successfully at the Keukenhof Garden in the Netherlands. Finally, remember that the colourful foliage of some varieties will extend the period of interest.

## Tulips as annuals

Tulips grown as spring bedding in municipal parks are a familiar sight. Typically, circular or rectangular beds are cut out of lawn and planted in a pattern using one or more tulip varieties and a carpet of a lower-growing plant. The result is impressive and uplifting in spring but it is an expensive way to use tulips and involves a lot of work. You may want to adapt the idea for your garden by using spring bedding on a small scale but where it will have a big impact on your day-to-day life. You could, for example, plant tulip bedding alongside the path to your front door or at the foot of a window. Small beds that are regularly viewed from indoors – such as those that are visible while you are washing up – are ideal candidates for spring bedding schemes.

## Perfect partners

When it comes to choosing partners for your tulips there are lots of possibilities and you can have great fun scanning bulb and seed catalogues and planning your plantings. One classic pairing is a froth of pale blue forget-me-nots punctuated with red tulips; for a more restful variation try pink, yellow or white tulips, or plant pink- or white-flowered forget-me-nots with a pink or white tulip.

Wallflowers offer warm hues of yellows, oranges and reds. Most are at their peak in late spring, so the late-season tulips like Queen of Night or Lily-flowered types work best. For the greatest impact, you will need a single-colour wallflower rather than a mixture, so it is worth growing your own from seed the previous summer.

**Left** The Lily-flowered tulip West Point stands to attention in front of an underplanting of dark blue grape hyacinths (*Muscari*). This is an easy combination that gives plenty of contrast and impact, although grape hyacinths can be rather invasive in mixed plantings.

**Right** Tulips arising from a mist of forget-me-nots is a plant combination that works well in all gardens from the grand to the small cottage garden. Here the intense colour of Red Parrot tulips adds richness and acts as a counterpoint to the pale blue beneath.

**Left** This spring border is packed with mid- and late-season tulips poised to take over from hellebores and other early spring-flowering plants. The mid-season tulip Arabian Mystery (purple with a white edge) is fully open while late varieties like the pink-flowered Esther are just emerging.

For a lower-growing partner to your tulips, there are plenty of options among the different-coloured polyanthus and pansies. For yellow tulips, a red polyanthus with a golden eye would be pleasing, whereas deep pink tulips would look better with pure white or pink. A drift of purple or blue pansies or violas would look great with any colour of tulip, but white tulips will help to make a small garden look bigger. Pick up on the maroon-mottled or striped foliage of the Greigii hybrids by teaming them with red double daisies (*Bellis perennis*) or a dark red pansy.

At renowned gardener Christopher Lloyd's garden at Great Dixter in Sussex, where there are many ideas for innovative plant combinations, tulips are paired with lupins. The emerging lupin foliage acts as a foil for the tulips, and when the tulip flowers are over, the lupins follow on. The lupins are pulled up and discarded after flowering and the bulbs harvested and stored when dormant.

## Tulips in containers

Tulips have the widest colour range of any of the spring bulbs, which makes them ideal for containers where they can be grown as single subjects or as part of a mixed planting.

Container growing also relieves you of having to prepare and plant in difficult soils such as heavy clay, and allows you to move pockets of spring colour to where they will have most impact. Pots of Double Early varieties like Peach Blossom or Willemsoord

can be given shelter in a cool conservatory, then taken outside when the weather is favourable. When the display is over, the containers can be whisked away. For a succession of spring colour on a patio, start with a container of Kaufmanniana or Greigii hybrids; when these are over, replace with a pot containing any early or mid-season tulip, and when that is past its best, bring on a tub of Lily-flowered or Parrot varieties.

Choose a large enough container and any tulip can be grown successfully, but if you are planting up small pots (under 30cm/12in diameter) or windowboxes in exposed locations it is best if you stick to the fairly short varieties, under 35cm/14in high – look among the Kaufmanniana, Fosteriana and Greigii

**Above** Wallflowers and tulips are a familiar and dependable pairing. Here they have been given a new twist by choosing them in warm orange tones not usually associated with spring. Grow dark orange wallflowers with a paler orange tulip like Prinses Irene or its double late sport, Orange Princess, for a similar effect.

types for candidates. Also, keep in mind the multiflowered types like Toronto and *T. praestans* 'Fusilier', which are both perfect for small containers. Good single subjects for larger pots near seats include tulips with unusual shapes or markings that are best appreciated close up: these include the Fringed, Parrot or Viridiflora types.

Ideas from spring bedding schemes can be scaled down and used in containers: tulips with an underplanting of dwarf wallflowers, double daisies, polyanthus, violas or grape hyacinths (*Muscari*), with flowers like tiny bunches of grapes, are easy ones to start with.

## Tulips as perennials

In countries, such as the UK, most of northern Europe and parts of the USA with hardy zones 3–8, tulips can be treated as perennials if they are planted deeply enough. However, in warmer climates, such as the southern states of the USA with hardy zones 9–10, only some species tulips like *T. bakeri* 'Lilac Wonder' are suitable for this treatment. (Here, it can even be difficult to grow tulips as annuals and the bulbs will usually need a cold treatment – store in a refrigerator in a paper bag – for 8–10 weeks prior to planting. They will also need to be planted deep and topped with a mulch to kept them cool.) Bulb catalogues from the relevant countries usually indicate those tulips that are good as perennials.

Treating tulips as perennials saves a lot of work. Take this one stage further and underplant with low-growing perennials rather than traditional spring bedding. Raid the rockery or alpine section of the garden centre for possible candidates such as aubrieta, *Aurinia saxatilis* (formerly *Alyssum saxatile*) or *Iberis sempervirens*. Aubrieta produces its purple flowers from early spring to early summer on mat-like plants, so can be grown with any season or height of tulip. *Aurinia saxatilis* is more bushy, up to 30cm (12in) high, and its yellow flowers appear in mid- to late spring, so choose the taller tulips and stick to mid- or late-season varieties. *Iberis sempervirens*, with its white flowers in mid- to late spring, only grows to 20cm (8in) high, so will suit almost any mid- to late-season tulip.

**Above** This stone planter filled with bright pink tulips, maroon wallflowers and dark blue forget-me-nots makes an impressive focal point. A similar effect could be obtained using a Single Late tulip like Pink Diamond.

**Opposite** A wooden barrel is deep enough to hold at least two layers of bulbs. Here, two varieties with the same flowering time but different heights have been chosen. A tall late variety like Blushing Lady could be paired with one of the smaller Lily-flowered tulips such as Maytime to create a similar combination.

**Above** The irises and geraniums in this mixed border have yet to flower but meanwhile tulips provide a bold splash of colour along with the sultry bells of *Fritillaria persica*. A tulip with a contrasting white edge adds extra drama amid the foliage. There are many white-edged examples to choose from among the Triumph tulips, such as Princess Victoria, Professor Penn or Valentine.

Another easy way to create a low-maintenance pairing is to grow tulips alongside dwarf shrubs – go for those with strong foliage colours and you will not have to worry about matching the flowering times. The best shrub for pairing with tulips must be a golden-leafed variety of the dwarf *Spiraea japonica*. Try 'Goldflame', which has orange tips to the young foliage in spring and makes a fiery scene with red or orange tulips. For a more subtle foil of blue-green, bright green or orange-brown, consider the wide range of dwarf hebes, while the yellow-green of the evergreen perennial *Euphorbia polychroma* reaches its peak in mid- to late spring, making it an ideal companion for mid- or late-season tulips in red, orange or purple.

Tulips will bring spring colour to bare ground near trees or large shrubs as long as the site receives sun for at least half the day.

Deciduous trees and shrubs let more light through than evergreens so, for example, under an apple tree you could plant late-season pink or white tulips and a carpet ground cover like silver-leafed deadnettle (*Lamium maculatum*). A bed with nothing but roses looks dull in spring, so brighten it up with an edging of dwarf tulips. Any of the smaller tulips would be suitable and they can be left in the ground year after year. Larger evergreens can be used as a foil for tulips; *Photinia* x *fraseri* 'Red Robin', for example, with its bright red new foliage, would make an exciting background for red or orange tulips.

## Tulips in borders

Mid- to late spring in a herbaceous border sees shoots poking up above the ground and low mounds of fresh green foliage forming over the bare earth. Add some tulips to this scene of awakening and from mid-spring onwards, the border will be alive with flowers and so will appear to be more advanced.

The wide colour palette of tulips offers unlimited scope. You could ring the changes with a totally different effect to the summer scheme – bold red-and-white Parrot tulips such as Estella Rijnveld preceding a summer border of pastels, for example. Alternatively, choose a hue that gives a taste of the colours to come, planting a yellow tulip like the early flowering Candela or the later-flowering Yellow Parrot as a precursor to a blue-and-yellow summer border, for example. The Single, Double Early, Double Late, Triumph, Darwin Hybrids, Parrot and Lily-flowered groups are most suitable for the middle and back of borders, while many of the smaller tulips such as the Greigii hybrids are ideal to use as edging.

**Below** Positioning these pink tulips near the emerging dark-leaved peony foliage makes an effective colour contrast but it has practical advantages too. As peonies do not need frequent lifting and dividing, the tulips can be left *in situ*. In the distance, is the white-and-green Spring Green tulip.

If you want your tulips to be left *in situ* year after year, place them near herbaceous plants that require the minimum of lifting and dividing, for example hostas or peonies. A green-and-white variegated hosta would look stunning with a late-flowering white tulip such as Mount Tacoma. For the best long-lived tulips, the foliage needs to be left to die down naturally so that it can feed the bulb ready for the following season. To disguise the unattractive

**Left** Under a deciduous tree, such as this Japanese maple, there is enough light and space for a medley of tulips. The soft colours of Apricot Beauty are contrasted with the dark purple of Maytime, an elegant Lily-flowered tulip.

fading bulb foliage, position the tulips in the middle or at the back of the border and at the front, accompany with plants that have camouflaging strap- or grass-like foliage, such as red hot pokers (*Kniphofia*) or the very lovely day lilies (*Hemerocallis*).

## Other planting possibilities
### Layering bulbs
Several layers of different spring bulbs with a range of flowering times can be planted either in the ground, in a raised bed or in a large pot. The pot will need to be at least 25cm/10in deep, and preferably deeper. This technique will extend the flowering season without taking up any more space or requiring a lot of pots to be moved to and fro. However, it can work out very expensive: approximately 150–200 bulbs will be needed for an area 1m (3ft) square.

Tulips in such schemes can be paired with another tulip (an early flowerer such as one of the Greigii or Kaufmannianas with a late-season tulip chosen from Single or Double Late, Lily-flowered or Parrot types), plus one or more of the earlier flowering smaller bulbs such as bulbous iris (*Iris reticulata*), crocus or dwarf daffodil. At the Keukenhof Garden in the Netherlands, for many years they have planted crocus on top of early tulips on top of late tulips, which ensures a sequence of colour from early to late spring. To plan your scheme, choose four or five subjects on the basis of their flowering time, height and how deeply they need to be planted.

### Winter pot plants
Growing prepared hyacinths is a tried and tested way of having flower colour indoors in the middle of winter. Certain tulip varieties can be planted in early autumn in the same way, although they need a longer cool period (around 12 weeks). You might try the particularly early Brilliant Star, as well as Apricot Beauty and Bellona. Use half a dozen bulbs per 15cm (6in) pot and pot them up in multipurpose or potting compost with their necks just below the surface. Water and keep in a cool, dark place to encourage rooting – a north-facing or shaded part of the garden where you can cover them with leafmould or peat is ideal. Once rooted, the bulb will produce top growth; when you see 8cm (3in) of top growth bring them indoors in a cool place but keep in the dark. The increase in temperature will lengthen the stems; once these are over 10cm (4in), move to a cool, light place to encourage the top growth to turn green.

### Unusual sites
A rockery, raised bed or alpine trough is the perfect home for the smaller species tulips that would be lost in larger mixed plantings. They may be rather shy to flower at first, but are very long lived.

Spring bulbs naturalized in grass between trees or on a slope also make a wonderful yet easy-to-maintain feature. Tulips are rarely naturalized in this way as their foliage is so large but some, such as *T. kaufmanniana* and its hybrids, are worth a try. Over the years, they will spread to create a carpet. You will need an area of grass where the first cut can be delayed until most of the bulb foliage has died back (about six weeks after flowering).

# buying, planting and maintenance

In autumn, packs of tulip bulbs are available in supermarkets and department stores, but for a greater range of varieties or if you want to choose your own loose bulbs – which makes them cheaper – you should visit a garden centre or garden stall in a market. For a specific variety or for large numbers of bulbs, buy from a specialist and be sure to place your order early in case they run out. When choosing your own tulip bulbs, pick out the best. Look for large, heavy bulbs, preferably 11cm (4½in) or 12cm (4¾in) – the bigger the bulb, the bigger the flower. The brown outer coating (the tunic) that protects the bulbs should be present and more or less intact. Reject any dried-out or chalky-looking bulbs as well as any with drops of what looks like brown glue on them – this is a sign that they have been in contact with 'sour' rot. However, the superficial blue mould on the tunic is not a problem so long as the bulbs are sound – simply rub the mould off and store the bulbs in a dry place until you plant them.

If you buy packets of bulbs, open them as soon as you get home, and remove and destroy any infected bulbs. Until you are ready to plant, store the bulbs spread out on a plastic or metal mesh tray in a cool, dry, dark place. (Note that handling tulip bulbs can bring some people out in an itchy rash, so if you have sensitive skin wear gloves. Tulip bulbs are listed as being poisonous if eaten so keep them out of reach of children.)

## Buying tulips as plants

Trays of potted tulip plants for sale with buds just showing colour are a tempting sight in spring. The advantage is that they have come through the winter unscathed and are certain to flower. Also, in spring you can see exactly where you want pockets of colour. There is a catch, of course: you will pay over the odds for them, and the choice of varieties will be limited. Smart gardeners can get around this by potting up bulbs in autumn so they are ready to plant out in spring.

## When and how to plant

Almost all spring-flowering bulbs should be planted in autumn, but tulips are an exception: they can be planted any time from mid-autumn to early winter. Late planting will still give an impressive display and the flowering will only lag by a week or two compared to bulbs planted earlier in the autumn. The ideal time is mid- to late autumn; any earlier and the emerging foliage in spring will be vulnerable to fungal disease and frost damage.

Tulips benefit from deep planting – a depth of 10cm (4in) is a minimum, 15cm (6in) is better. Even deeper planting (20–25cm/8–10in) means you can leave the bulbs in the ground and plant summer bedding on top. Sometimes it is not possible to plant deeply – if the topsoil is shallow for example, or you have hundreds of bulbs to plant and little time. In such circumstances shallow planting at 5–8cm (2–3in) will suffice if you only want to treat the tulips as annuals.

A bulb planter or a large dibber made from an old wooden spade handle will make planting quicker and easier than using a trowel. For large-scale planting or for planting into turf, use a long-handled planter. Alternatively cut the turf with a half-moon cutter or sharp spade and roll it back. Few bulb planters go deep enough for bulbs that are to be left in the ground for several years: in this case you will need to use a spade.

## The right place

As long as the bulb does not rot in a waterlogged soil over winter, you are more or less guaranteed a tulip, whatever the soil or site. That said, a position with light from all sides will produce straighter stems, which is important in the taller varieties, while blooms will be retained longer in a sheltered site.

However, if you want to keep your bulbs from one year to the next, planting in the right place becomes much more important. Tulips do best on a free-draining garden loam, in a spot that is warm and dry over the summer when the bulbs are dormant – this usually means a sunny position, but they can cope with partial shade. If you have problems with waterlogging, you may be able to improve drainage by digging in garden compost or grit but large quantities will be needed, so consider growing tulips in raised beds of free-draining topsoil or in containers instead.

## Beds and borders

Choose a sunny site in the border, the further back the better so that the emerging perennials will hide the dying tulip foliage in early summer. Scatter the bulbs around randomly, either in groups of 20 or more for a cluster of colour or in a drift that snakes in and out of other plants.

Make a hole and place one bulb in it, with its pointed end uppermost. Replace the soil on top of the bulb and firm it down gently with your hands. To layer bulbs, use a spade to dig out an area 1m (3ft) square and 20cm (8in) deep, plant the first layer of bulbs, cover with soil, plant the next layer, and so on.

When planting a formal spring bedding scheme, mark out the area to be planted and set out all the bedding first, spacing it about 30cm (12in) apart – 15cm (6in) for the small types and dwarf varieties. Plant the bedding, then set out and plant the tulips, usually 15cm (6in) apart.

## Rows

A straight line of tulips standing to attention looks very striking in a formal garden, especially if you have a narrow bed alongside an evergreen hedge or wall. Growing in rows also makes sense when tulips are grown for cutting; these can be set out in the vegetable patch or on an allotment. If you do opt to grow tulips as cut flowers, the Triumph and Darwin Hybrids are those used commercially, but it is worth considering the more unusual or expensive subjects like the Lily-flowered, Viridiflora or Parrot tulips. To prevent the build-up of soil-borne diseases, incorporate tulips into a three-year crop rotation – tulips do well on ground that has grown potatoes the year before.

To plant a row of tulips, use a garden line to mark out a straight line. Dig a trench at least three times the height of the bulb and space out the bulbs evenly along the bottom, leaving 5–15cm (2–6in) between them, depending on variety. Cover the bulbs with soil and firm the ground with your foot. Finally, label the trench.

## Aftercare

After planting, little aftercare is needed apart from watering if the soil is very dry, unless you have problems with mice, squirrels, pests and diseases (see below), or if you want the bulbs to flower in future years. If this is the case and there has been a lot of heavy rain over the winter and you have a free-draining soil, apply a feed as growth gets underway. One low in nitrogen but rich in potash would be suitable – either a proprietary bulb fertilizer for use in spring or a tomato feed once a week after flowering until the leaves die down. If the soil is fairly fertile you can get away without feeding. Remove the faded flowers immediately after flowering to direct the plant's energy back down into the bulb.

When the foliage has died down, lift the bulbs, dry them and clean to remove any soil, then store in a well-ventilated place until you replant in mid- to late autumn. If the foliage has not yet died down and the tulips are in the way of the summer bedding, either replant in another part of the garden so the leaves can die down naturally or go straight on to drying and storing them.

## Container plantings

Containers should be at least 30cm (12in) across and deep, although 20–25cm (8–10in) would do for species tulips. The tulips are normally planted more densely than in the ground, so are best discarded each year, in which case use your preferred potting mix. Place a generous layer of crocks over the drainage holes and add compost to a depth of 10cm (4in) or so. Position the tulip bulbs, starting in the centre and working outwards; they can be very close but not touching. Cover with more potting compost so the tips of the bulbs are just showing. Now plant the underplanting (or another layer of bulbs), and this time fill in the spaces around the edge of the pot. Add more compost to 2.5–5cm (1–2in) below the rim, firm down and water well. Water regularly once the leaves start to grow. If you want to keep the bulbs for planting out in the garden next year, liquid feed when the leaves are growing strongly and again as the buds form.

## Tulip problems

This list looks daunting, but you are unlikely to experience more than one of these problems in any one year.

**Droppers** These are swollen, root-like structures that grow from the top of the bulb down into the soil. Eventually, a new bulb will form lower down and flower after a couple of years. Droppers occur if bulbs are planted too shallow or if the soil dries out too much.

**Eelworm** This causes the stems to bend, the leaves to split and the petals to stay green. The bulbs were probably infested prior to planting or the eelworm was in the soil and entered through a small wound. When the plant dies, the eelworm will move on to other plants so dig up and burn any infested plants promptly. To prevent the problem, buy from a reputable supplier and reject any soft bulbs.

**Greenfly (aphids)** Bulbs in storage can be infested and damage can continue once they are in the ground. Spray with insecticide.

**Mice** Bulbs in store or in the ground may be nibbled. Try a covering over the ground of wire netting (mesh size no more than 1cm/½in) or of prickly leaves like holly. Indoors, set traps.

**Poor flowering** In time, tulip bulbs form clumps of smaller bulbs around them known as offsets. If left, the tulips will decline or even not flower at all, so separate and remove some of the offsets when the bulbs are lifted.

**Root and foot rot** These are caused by soil-borne fungi. The base of the stem decays and the rot spreads through the plant. Remove and destroy infected plants and ensure garden hygiene by removing decaying plant debris and always using a clean source when watering.

**Slugs and snails** These cause holes in leaves, stems, flowers or even bulbs. Growing bulbs in containers or raised beds helps reduce the risk, plus checking nightly to remove any offenders. You may need to resort to slug pellets; follow the instructions on the packet to minimize the danger to wildlife. For a precious tulip collection, watering on a suitable biological control is worth trying, but this can be expensive over a large area.

**Squirrels** In gardens where squirrels abound, protect bulbs over winter. A covering of chicken wire secured at the edges works well.

**Tulip fire** A form of botrytis (grey mould), the symptoms are a brown scorching of the young foliage, followed by sooty specks on the leaves and flowers. Remove and burn infected leaves immediately, and spray the remaining foliage with a suitable systemic fungicide.

**Virus** Tulip breaking virus still occurs sporadically and the first you will see of it is a plain-coloured tulip breaking into white or yellow streaks. The virus is spread by aphids and is more prevalent among late-flowering varieties. Once a plant has the virus there is little you can do to stop the spread, except remove and destroy the plant – although you might want to keep it if you like the pattern!

# Index

# Suppliers

## USA

Brent and Becky's Bulbs
7463 Heath Trail
Gloucester VA 23061
Tel: +1 804 693 3966
www.brentandbeckysbulbs.com

Bloms Bulbs Inc
491-233 Glen Eagle Square
Glen Mills PA 19342
Tel: +1 866 7 TULIPS
www.blomsbulbs.com

McClure and Zimmerman
108 W. Winnebago St
PO Box 368
Friesland WI 53935–0368
Tel: +1 800 883 6998
www.mzbulb.com

John Scheepers Inc
23 Tulip Drive
Bantam CT 06750
Tel: +1 860 567 0838
www.johnscheepers.com

Van Bourgondien
PO Box 1000, Babylon
New York 11702
Tel: +1 800 622 9959
www.dutchbulbs.com

Washington Bulb Co Inc
*See Roozengaarde under Show Gardens*

White Flower Farm
30 Irene St
Torrington CT 06790
Tel: +1 800 503 9624
www.whiteflowerfarm.com

## UK

Jacques Amand
The Nurseries
145 Clamp Hill
Stanmore
Middlesex HA7 3JS
Tel: +44 (0) 20 8420 7110
*Their range includes hard-to-find and unusual tulips*

Avon Bulbs
Burnt House Farm
Mid-Lambrook
South Petherton
Somerset TA13 5HE
Tel: +44 (0)1460 242177
www.avonbulbs.co.uk

Bloms Bulbs Ltd
Primrose Nurseries
Melchbourne
Beds MK44 1ZZ
Tel: +44 (0)1234 709099
www.blomsbulbs.com

Peter Nyssen Ltd
124 Flixton Rd
Urmston
Manchester M41 5BG
Tel: +44 (0)161 747 4000
E-mail
peternyssenltd@btinternet.com
*Minimum order 50 of any variety*

## NETHERLANDS

Bijzondere Bloembollen
Postbus 653
2100 AR Heemstede
Tel: +31 (0) 252 530 353

Bloembollen Kwekerij
De Boender 6
2204 AG Nordwijk
Tel: +31 (0) 252 372193

Tulip World BV
Grasweg 71
1031 HX Amsterdam
www.tulipworld.com
*Modern-looking website offering an on-line bulb store and design and style ideas for using tulips*

Van Tubergen
Postbus 144
8250 AC Dronten
Tel: +31 (0) 321 385141
E-mail tuber@oranjebandzaden.nl

Walter Blom & Zoon BV
Hyacinthenlaan 2
2182 DE Hillegrom
Tel: +31 (0) 252 519444
www.blomsbulbs.com

## GERMANY

Blumenzwiebel Import und Grosshandel
Postfach 1270
D–27342 Rotenburg/Wümme
Tel: +49 (0) 42 6163818

Dipl Ing Gardenbau
Fasanenweg 23
D–21717 Fredenbeck
Tel: +49 (0) 41 491640

Pflanzenspezialitäten
Potsdamer Strasse 40
D–14163 Berlin
Tel: +49 (0) 0 80 26251

Samengrosshandlung
Berliner Strasse 88
D–14169 Berlin
Tel: +49 (0) 30 81 14304

## FRANCE

Baumaux
BP 100
54062 Nancy Cedex
Tel: +33 (0) 383 158 686
www.graines-baumaux.fr

Bulbes d'Opale
384 Boerenweg Ouest
59285 Buysscheure
Tel: +33 (0) 328 430 467

Ellebore
La Chamotière
61360 St-Jouin-de-Blavou
Tel: +33 (0) 233 833 772

Schryve Jardin
1315 route du Stent'je
59270 Bailleul
Tel: +33 (0) 328 492 740

## AUSTRALIA/ NEW ZEALAND

Van Eeden Tulips
Dept G, West Plains Rd, 4RD
Invercargill
New Zealand
Tel: +64 (0) 3 215 7836
E-mail:
vaneedentulips@xtra.co.nz

New Gippsland Seeds and Bulbs
PO Box 1
Silvan
Victoria 3795
Australia
Tel: +61 (0) 3 9737 9560

# Societies

International Bulb Society
PO Box 92136
Pasadena, CA 91109–2136
USA

Wakefield and North of England Tulip Society
70 Wrenthorpe Lane
West Yorkshire WF2 0PT
*A society that keeps the florist tulip legacy alive via its annual journal, meetings and shows.*

# Show Gardens

Keukenhof
Stationweg 166A
2161 AM Lisse
Netherlands
www.keukenhof.nl

Cambridge University Botanic Garden
Cory Lodge
Bateman St
Cambridge CB2 1JF
England
Tel: +44 (0) 1223 336265
*National Collection of tulips*

Roozengaarde
PO Box 1248
Mount Vernon, WA 98273
USA
Tel: +1 866 488 5477
www.tulips.com
*Show garden and supplier of fresh flowers and bulbs via Washington Bulb Co Inc*

## Author's Acknowledgements

I would like to thank Cees Breed for his help in selecting the tulips featured in this book, for providing information on their origin and for patiently answering my queries. My thanks also extend to Clay Perry whose photographs have captured the essence of each variety so perfectly.

My interest in tulips first arose while I was working for *Gardening which?* magazine. Here I had the opportunity to visit tulip trials and the gardens of keen tulip growers; I will always remember the dedication and enthusiasm of Wendy Akers and her daughter Sarah Wainwright for the English tulips. My thanks also extend to the staff at the Royal Horticultural Society Library at Vincent Square, London.

It has been a real pleasure to work with the staff at Quadrille, in particular Hilary Mandleberg, the Project Editor, for her support and encouragement from start to finish.


## Photographer's Acknowledgements

The photographer would like to thank the following: Marylyn Abbott, West Green House, Hartley Wintney, Hampshire; the Directors of the Keukenhof Garden, Lisse, Holland; Stanley Killingback, South Woodford, London; Peter Lloyd, Highgate, London; Jim Sellick, Pashley Manor, East Sussex; Maureen Thompson, Long Melford, Suffolk.